Social Media Mastery: Sealing the Deal with Your Dream Client

Betty T. Vargas

TABLE OF CONTENT

Chapter 1

Crafting a Captivating Online Presence

Presenting your own personality and value offer is the key to creating an irresistible personal brand. To create an engaging personal brand, follow these essential steps:

Define Your Identity: - Clearly state your beliefs, interests, and capabilities. Determine what makes you unique among the others in your profession.

Write an Intriguing Brand Narrative:
 Write a story that explains your goals and path. Emphasize significant events that helped to form your professional persona.

Establish a Uniform Visual Identity: - Create a polished logo by utilizing standardized colors and typefaces.

Make sure the personality of your brand is reflected in the visual aspects.

Optimize Online Presence: -
Create a compelling LinkedIn profile that includes a headshot and extensive bio.
 Select and disseminate stuff that is relevant to your experience and passions.

Engage Authentically:-
Make a real connection with your audience.
React to messages and comments as soon as possible.

Showcase Expertise:-
Use blog entries, articles, or videos to impart your knowledge.
Become recognized as an expert in your area.

Strategic Networking: - Participate in business gatherings and establish connections with experts.
Build ties with influencers and opinion leaders.

Seek Feedback and Adapt:-
Evaluate the performance of your brand on a regular basis and make any adjustments.
Solicit comments from coworkers, mentors, or peers.

Deliver Consistent Quality: - Make sure that the caliber of your work is continuously in line with the brand.
Fulfill or above expectations to foster confidence.

Evolve Over Time:-
Adapt your personal brand to suit with your developing goals and experiences.
 Accept change and keep honing your brand as you expand.

Recall that building an enticing personal brand is a continuous process that advances together with your professional life. Maintain your authenticity while making adjustments to your industry's shifting needs.

For your social media presence to leave a lasting impression, optimization is essential. The following actions are crucial to achieving optimal effect:

Profile Photo:- Make sure your profile image accurately represents your personal brand and is professional.
 Make sure the background is clear and your face is well-lit.

Username and Handle: - Pick a username or handle that complements your own brand. Maintain consistency across all platforms to facilitate recognition.

Bio and About Section - Write a succinct and interesting bio that emphasizes your areas of expertise and passions.
Add pertinent keywords to improve discoverability.

Contact Information: - Include links to your expert website or correct contact information. Make it simple for users to get in touch with you outside the platform.

Link to Website or Portfolio:- Provide a link to your professional website, blog, or portfolio. Point visitors to a central repository for your accomplishments and efforts.

Edit Banners and Headers:
 Make use of visually striking banners that complement your brand.
Add your slogan or a succinct description of what you have to offer.

Content Showcase:- Feature key or noteworthy content at the top of your account.
Make sure you prominently display your greatest work, accomplishments, or testimonials.

Follow Relevant Accounts: - Follow peers, organizations, and leaders in the sector.

Interact with their material to increase your exposure.

Privacy Settings:- Examine and modify privacy settings in accordance with your tastes.
 Strike a balance between comfort and visibility in the workplace.

Coherent Branding: - Ensure that your visual identity is consistent across all platforms.
To maintain brand consistency, use comparable typefaces, colors, and message.

Regular Updates: - Make sure your profile details are current.
Share current successes, initiatives, or insights periodically.

Involve Your Audience: - Quickly reply to messages and comments.
Interact with other people's material to promote a feeling of community.

You may improve the effect of your personal brand, create a lasting impression, and increase your online presence by using these tactics to optimize your social media profiles.

One important tactic to demonstrate your ***knowledge is to curate interesting information. Here's how to produce captivating content for your audience:***

Know Your Audience: - Determine the interests of your intended audience.
 Modify your material to suit their interests and requirements.

Explain Your Specialization:- Clearly state what your area of expertise is.
Concentrate on writing that showcases your special abilities and expertise.

 Remain Educated:

Keep up with news and developments in the business.
Provide your audience with up-to-date and pertinent information.

Create Valuable Content: - Offer insightful and useful information.
Provide solutions or tackle issues that your audience frequently encounters.

Diversify Content Types: - Include videos, infographics, and photos in addition to text-based postings.
Make an effort to accommodate your audience's varying learning styles.

Tell Compelling Stories:- Share personal experiences or case studies.
Write stories that your readers can relate to.

Utilize Visual Elements:- Enhance your text with visually appealing images.
Make use of excellent pictures, graphs, or charts.

Promote Interaction:– Make inquiries to start conversations.
 React to remarks and promote a feeling of community.

Regular publishing Schedule:– To ensure consistency, set up a regular publishing schedule.
 Determine the best times to post by using analytics.

Support Collaboration: - Work together with other authorities or influential people. Highlight guest pieces or take part in collaborative initiatives.

Share Success Stories: - Highlight your accomplishments and noteworthy experiences. Provide examples of the observable results of your experience.

Educational information: - Provide instruction manuals, instructions, or information on how-tos.
Present yourself as an invaluable source of knowledge.

Adapt to Feedback: - Consider what the audience has to say.
Modify your content strategy in light of the most effective elements.

Always remember that the secret is to interact with your audience sincerely and regularly offer value. You establish yourself as a trustworthy authority in your industry by selecting material that both demonstrates your competence and caters to the demands of your audience.

Chapter 2

Strategic Networking Strategies

Choosing and focusing on your ideal customer requires a calculated strategy. This is a handbook to assist you in identifying and connecting with your ideal clientele:

Define Your Perfect Client Profile: - List attributes such as industry, size of organization, location, and demographics.
 Take into account the problems your services can help with.

Research Your Niche:- Recognize the particular requirements and problems that your target industry faces.
Remain up to date on innovations and trends in the sector.

Create Buyer Personas:- Construct thorough profiles that reflect your target clientele. Provide details about their objectives, difficulties, and decision-making procedures.

Use Social Media Insights: - Comprehend your present audience by utilizing social media analytics.
 Determine the characteristics that your current clientele share.

Networking at Industry Events:- Participate in seminars, conferences, and networking gatherings.
 Establish connections with professionals in the sector and prospective clients.

Watch Online Discussions:- Engage in social media groups and forums pertaining to your sector.
 Pay attention to conversations to ascertain wants and worries.

Competitor Analysis: - Examine the clientele of your rivals.
Determine any gaps or places in which you can offer special assistance.

Create Thought Leadership - Distribute your knowledge via webinars, publications, and blogs.
Establish yourself as a recognized expert in your area.

Improve Your Value Proposition - Clearly state the special value that you provide.
Match your offerings to the particular requirements of your ideal customers.

Make Use of SEO Techniques - Make sure your web content is optimized for pertinent keywords.
Make sure your target audience can find your website with ease.

Participate in Direct Outreach - Write customized letters to prospective customers.

Emphasize how your offerings may help them with their particular problems.

Create Strategic Alliances: Work together with companies that serve your intended market. Look for collaborations that might benefit both parties.

Customer Referrals:- Motivate happy customers to recommend you to others. Use gratifying testimonies to establish trustworthiness.

Assess and Modify:- Consistently determine how well your targeted tactics are working. Modify your strategy in response to criticism and performance indicators.

You may more successfully discover and target your ideal clientele by combining these tactics, which will raise the possibility of deep and fruitful collaborations.

Developing a reputation via powerful relationships is crucial for career *advancement.* *Here's a how-to for efficiently using powerful connections:*

Identify Key Influencers: - Find influential people in your field or sector.
Look for people with a strong web presence, knowledge, or a huge following.

Integrate Genuinely: - Connect with and follow influencers on social media.
Leave intelligent comments on their blogs and provide them pertinent links.

Add Value to Conversations: - Incorporate insightful commentary into conversations.
Provide your knowledge without coming out as self-serving.

Attend Industry Events: - Go to networking gatherings, seminars, and workshops.
 Take the opportunity to engage with influencers in person.

Collaborate on Projects: - Make the suggestion to work together on initiatives or projects. Emphasize the advantages of collaboration for both parties.

Offer Assistance: - Give freely of your expertise and assistance.
When applicable, provide guidance or advice.

Request Mentoring: - Suggestively ask for advice or a mentor.
Clearly state how their experience fits with your objectives.

Share Their Content: - Disseminate content from influencers to your social media circles. To promote recognition, tag them in pertinent postings.

Generate Win-Win Circumstances:
Look for chances when everyone wins. Make partnerships that will increase the influencer's and your own credibility.

Create sincere connections:
Put your energy into creating sincere, lasting connections.
0Genuine relationships give rise to more significant teamwork.

Celebrate Their Success- Openly recognize and honor the influencer's accomplishments.
Express your admiration for what they have contributed to the field.

Establish Yourself as a Resource:- Use your own content to highlight your areas of expertise.
Present yourself to others as an invaluable resource.

Attend Exclusive Events: - Take part in gatherings or forums that include prominent people.
Making meaningful relationships might result from networking in certain groups.

Remain Current:

Keep up with the influencer's activities and pursuits.
Engage in conversations that connect with their present activity.

Express Gratitude:- Thank you for any assistance or guidance you have received.
 Always speak with a kind and upbeat attitude.

Utilizing powerful connections necessitates a sincere strategy that emphasizes relationship-building above transactional networking. Your credibility in the eyes of your professional community will inevitably rise as you foster these ties.

Reaching out effectively is essential to genuine *participation. These are tried-and-true methods to include in your outreach plan:*

Research Your Target:
 - Learn about the hobbies and background of the receiver.
   Tailor your appeal to their particular need.

Write an Intriguing Sentence:
Compose a succinct and unique message.
- Clearly state the benefits you offer and the reasons it matters to them.

Create a Common Ground
- Look for connections or areas of interest in common.
- Bring up shared connections, experiences, or ties.

Highlight Prior Interactions:
- Make mention of any prior meetings or discussions.
Remind them of your good interactions to establish a sense of familiarity.

Offer Value Up Front:
- Make sure they understand the advantages.
- Illustrate how your suggestion fits with their objectives or difficulties.

Use a Clear Call-to-Action:

- Clearly articulate the actions you suggest as the next stages.
   - Make it simple for them to reply or act.

Make Use of Social Proof:
- Bring up pertinent successes, endorsements, or awards.
   - Provide proof of your accomplishments and reputation.

Customize Your Subject Lines:
   - Write headlines that pique readers' interest and draw them in.
   Steer clear of topic lines that seem like spam.

Timing Is Important:
 - Send outreach during times when your target audience is most receptive.
   - Take work schedules and time zones into account.

Strategic Follow-Up:
 - Write brief and courteous follow-up communications.

- Exhibit perseverance without becoming unduly insistent.

Utilize Multiple Channels:
 - Make use of social media, email, and professional networks in combination.
 - Modify your strategy according to the platform that the recipient prefers.

Be Concise:
 - Make sure your outreach message is succinct and direct.
 - Grab their attention without giving them too much information.

Express Sincere Interest:
- Demonstrate a sincere interest in their accomplishments or body of work.
 Steer clear of template-based or general outreach.

Create a Relationship:
- Put more emphasis on building a relationship than on quick deals.

- Devote time to developing connections in order to foster sustained involvement.

Test Your Strategy A/B:
- Test out various outreach techniques.
Determine which strategies produce the greatest results, then make the necessary adjustments.

You may raise the possibility of meaningful interaction and create enduring relationships with your target audience by putting these outreach strategies into practice. Recall that effective outreach depends on communication that is both individualized and value-driven.

Chapter 3

Closing the Deal: From Connection to Contract

It takes careful planning to navigate digital communication effectively. The following tactics can help you improve your digital communication:

Conciseness and Clarity:- Clearly state your point in a succinct manner.
Steer clear of superfluous jargon and convoluted terminology.

Use Appropriate Tone:- Adjust your tone according to the audience and circumstance.

Act politely, professionally, and situationally as
necessary.

Select the Correct Channel: - Decide on the
best channel for communication.
Certain circumstances can call for video calls,
direct messaging, or emails.

Active Listening:- Pay attention to what people
have to say before answering.
To promote understanding, acknowledge their
arguments and respond to them.

Adopt Visual Communication:- Use images to
improve comprehension.
Use visuals, charts, and infographics where
applicable.

Consider Your Timing: - Pay attention to
timetables and time zones.
  Plan digital communications during times that
work best for everyone.

Promote Feedback: - Establish channels for candid criticism and discussion.
Encourage an atmosphere in which people are at ease sharing their thoughts.

Be Aware of Words: - Select inclusive words to show consideration for various audiences.
 Steer clear of any terminology that might be seen as discriminatory or insulting.

Make Wise Use of Emojis and GIFs: - Emojis and GIFs may be used to express tone and emotions.
   Keep in mind that they might not be acceptable in certain professional settings.

Create Engaging material:
- Write captivating material for your readers.
   - To increase the impact of your messages, employ narrative tactics.

Respect Response Time:
- Be considerate of others' preferences for response times and times.

- Make sure that response time expectations are understood.

Protect Communication Channels:
- Guarantee that communication channels are secure.
- For sensitive information, use encrypted platforms.

Adjust to Diverse Cultures:
 - Recognize and adjust to cultural quirks in discourse.
    - To prevent misunderstandings, learn about cultural conventions.

Use Hyperlinks Judiciously:
- Insert hyperlinks for extra information.
    - Make sure the linkages advance comprehension and maintain their relevance.

Edit and proofread:
    - Check for mistakes in your digital correspondence.

Communicate with poise and professionalism by using messages that are well written.

These tactics can help you create meaningful and productive digital communication practices that will promote successful interactions. ***Recall to be flexible and mindful of the variety of internet communication.***

To successfully navigate discussions and achieve desired results, confidence is a need. The following are ***techniques to improve your ability to negotiate***:

Research and Preparation:
- Investigate the topic and the persons concerned in great detail.
   Be well-prepared by anticipating any objections and concerns.

Set Clearly Defined Objectives:
 - Specify your priorities and aims for the discussion.

- Clearly state your objectives for the conversation.

Understand Your Value:
 - Acknowledge and express your own worth throughout the bargaining process.
 - Clearly state how your suggestion will help each and every person.

Active Listening:
- Pay close attention to what the other person has to say.
 - Recognize their wants and worries in order to establish a common ground.

Efficient Communication:
 - Clearly state your ideas and suggestions.
 - Speak in an aggressive but courteous manner.

Consider Instead of Arguing:
 - Pay attention to identifying win-win solutions.
 Steer clear of conflicts and strive for agreement.

Remain Calm and Composed:
  - Retain your calm even in trying circumstances.
   - Your decision-making and believability are improved by maintaining composure.

Adaptability and Flexibility - Be willing to modify your strategy in light of fresh knowledge.
   Adjust to shifting conditions during the bargaining process.

Create Win-Win Solutions:
  - Look for solutions that are advantageous to all stakeholders.
   Encourage a cooperative environment as opposed to a competitive one.

Establish a rapport:
   - Build a solid rapport with the other side.
   Establishing trust is a must for fruitful negotiations.

Know When to Walk Away: - Recognize your boundaries and when it's time to give up.

   - Your negotiation position might be strengthened if you are prepared to give up.

Make the Most of Silence: - Welcome times of quiet during the discussion.

   Give the opposing side time to think things out and react.

Document Agreements: - During talks, clearly record the conditions that were agreed upon.

   - Having a documented record helps to prevent misunderstandings.

Be Patient:- Be persistent and patient since negotiations may take some time.

   Rushing may result in less than ideal results.

Ongoing Education: - Contemplate about every negotiating encounter and extract knowledge from it.

   - Over time, consistently improve your negotiating techniques.

A strategic mentality, ***good communication, and preparation are all necessary for approaching talks with confidence.*** You may negotiate with confidence and raise your chances of getting what you want out of the deal by using these tactics.

Strategic activities are needed to close a deal resulting ***from social media engagement. Here's how to transform those exchanges into fruitful partnerships:***

Create Relationship Foundations:
- Foster sincere bonds by persistent involvement
  - Prioritize establishing a rapport before requesting cooperation.

Identify Mutual Benefits:
 - Clearly state how working together will benefit both sides.
   - Stress how the collaboration advances shared objectives.

Showcase Your Value:
- Emphasize your advantages, skills, and specialties.
   - Show how your efforts will improve the team's collaboration.

Pitch with Precision:
- Create a unique and persuasive pitch.
   - Customize your proposal to the prospective partner's unique requirements and preferences.

Make Use of Past exchanges:
 - Make reference to successful social media engagements and exchanges.
   - Bring up conversations or common interests that point to synergy.

Make Use of Direct Messaging:
 - Start a private discussion to talk about working together.
   - Remain courteous, succinct, and value-focused in your communication.

Provide Social Proof:
 - Provide endorsements or instances of fruitful partnerships.
   - Highlight the ways in which working with you has helped others.

Offer Trials or Test Periods:
 - Offer a trial time to see how well cooperation works.
   - Show off your expertise and dedication.

Align Branding Efforts:
- Make sure that messaging and branding are consistent.
   - Project a cohesive image to increase the legitimacy of the collaboration.

Enter into negotiations Transparently: -Express clear expectations about deliveries and pay.
   Steer clear of surprises and cultivate open communication to build trust.

Examine Cross-Promotion:

- Make suggestions for reciprocal promotion on one another's social media accounts.

   - Expand your reach by taking use of each other's audiences.

Celebrate Milestones Together:
- Work together to commemorate occasions, accomplishments, or landmarks.

   - Strengthen the alliance with mutually beneficial outcomes.

Address Concerns Promptly:
- Respond to any issues or queries that are brought up.

   - Respond quickly to problems in order to keep the connection going well.

Formalize Agreements:
- Write a precise and thorough partnership agreement.

   Make sure that all conditions, obligations, and duties are specified.

Express Gratitude:

- Thank them for their cooperation and thoughtfulness.
  - Remain thankful and upbeat throughout the bargaining process.

Establishing lucrative partnerships through social media interactions necessitates a careful balancing act between communicating clearly, establishing relationships, and providing value. You may successfully move from online contacts to fruitful collaborations by using these tactics.

Some point where repeated for emphasis

Case Study: From Connection to Collaboration

Get to know Jane, a Marketing Expert:

Jane, an experienced marketing practitioner, used the techniques described in "Social Media Mastery" to turn a chance social media encounter into a profitable partnership. She demonstrated her skills and cultivated deep connections by deliberately interacting with her ideal clientele on social media channels.

Creating an Alluring Digital Image:
 - Jane updated her LinkedIn page, emphasizing her major accomplishments and marketing knowledge.
 - She established herself as a thought leader by continuously sharing insightful articles about business trends.

Tactical Networking Techniques:
 - Jane followed important influencers and interacted with their material.
 She built a relationship with her target audience by making insightful remarks and sharing them.

Sealing the Agreement: From Relationship to Agreement:
 As soon as the chance presented itself, Jane sent out a direct message indicating her desire to work with someone.

- By employing her acquired negotiating abilities, she effectively conveyed the shared advantages of the collaboration.

What was the outcome? Jane was able to secure a contract with her ideal customer by skillfully transforming her social media interactions into a cooperative project. This case study shows how the techniques described in "Social Media Mastery" may be used in practical situations to assist professionals in confidently navigating the digital world and achieving measurable economic success.

Another Example: Sarah, the Freelance Consultant

In the book, we follow Sarah, a freelance consultant seeking to secure high-profile clients in her niche through social media mastery. Here's a glimpse into her journey:

Crafting an Irresistible Online Presence:

- Sarah strategically revamps her LinkedIn profile, optimizing her headline and summary to showcase her expertise in a compelling way.

- She incorporates a professional yet engaging profile picture and a banner that reflects her personal brand.

Strategic Networking Strategies:

- Leveraging the insights from the book, Sarah identifies key industry influencers on Twitter and engages with their content.

- Through meaningful interactions, she builds a rapport with these influencers, laying the groundwork for potential collaborations.

Closing the Deal: From Connection to Contract:

- Drawing from the negotiation strategies in the book, Sarah initiates private conversations with potential clients who have shown interest in her services.

- She adeptly navigates these discussions, addressing concerns, showcasing her value, and ultimately turning connections into lucrative contracts.

Another Example: John, the E-commerce Entrepreneur

Consider another example, this time focusing on John, an e-commerce entrepreneur seeking to expand his business through social media:

Crafting an Irresistible Online Presence:
   - John optimizes his business's Instagram profile by curating visually appealing content that highlights product offerings.
   - He utilizes Instagram Stories to provide behind-the-scenes glimpses, showcasing the human side of his brand.

Strategic Networking Strategies:
   - John actively engages with potential customers and industry influencers on Facebook groups related to his niche.
   - By participating in relevant discussions, he establishes his brand as a trusted authority in the e-commerce space.

Closing the Deal: From Connection to Contract:
   - Building on the negotiation insights from the book, John tactfully approaches influencers for product collaborations.
   - Through effective communication, he secures partnerships that not only boost brand visibility but also result in increased sales.

These examples provide a snapshot of how individuals in different business contexts can apply the principles outlined in "Social Media Mastery: Sealing the Deal with Your Dream Client" to achieve success in their social media endeavors.

9 798876 020666